A CULTURAL MOSAIC

A STUDY OF THE DIVERSE TRADITIONS AND CUSTOMS OF INDIA

DR. JAGADEESH PILLAI

|| "Dedicated to all who seek to understand and appreciate Indian culture and tradition." ||

Contents

Contents

Prayer

"Om Poornamadah Poornamidam Poornat
Poornamudachyate,Poornasya Poornamaadaya
Poornamevavashishyate,Om Shantih, Shantih, Shantih"

*The literal interpretation of this mantra is: That which is
Absolute, This which is Absolute, Absolute arises from Absolute,
If Absolute is removed from Absolute, Absolute remains
OM Peace, Peace, Peace.*

ॐॐॐ

About The Author

Dr. Jagadeesh Pillai is a renowned Guinness World Record holder, writer, and researcher hailing from Varanasi, also known as the abode of Lord Shiva. With a Ph.D. in Vedic Science and a range of creative ideas and achievements, he is a true polymath. He is the author of more than 100 books including Research Publications. Although his roots can be traced back to Kerala, the people of Varanasi hold him in high regard and affectionately consider him one of their own.

Dr. Pillai has achieved four Guinness World Records in the following subjects:

"Script to Screen" - In this record, Dr. Pillai produced and directed an animation film within the shortest time possible, breaking the previous record set by Canadians. He has also received numerous national and international awards and recognitions for this achievement.

Longest Line of Postcards - For this record, Dr. Pillai created a line of 16,300 postcards on the occasion of the 163rd anniversary of Indian Postal Day. The event also included a questionnaire about the Indian flag.

Largest Poster Awareness Campaign - Dr. Pillai designed an awareness campaign on the subject of "Beti Bachao - Beti Padhao" (Save the Girl Child - Educate the Girl Child) to achieve this record.

Largest Envelope - In tribute to the Indian Prime Minister's

"Make in India" initiative, Dr. Pillai created a 4000 square meter envelope using waste paper to achieve this record.

Attempted - **70000 Candles on a 210 kg Cake** - To celebrate the 70th Indian Independence Day, Dr. Pillai attempted to light 70,000 candles on a 210 kg cake, which was recorded in World Records India.

Attempted - **Documentary on Dhamek Stupa of Sarnath in 17 Languages** - Dr. Pillai attempted to create a documentary on the Dhamek Stupa of Sarnath, dubbing it in 17 different languages. The result of this attempt is currently awaiting confirmation from the Guinness World Records.

Dr. Pillai is skilled in teaching the Bhagavad Gita, a Hindu scripture, and is popular among young people. He has helped many young people improve their lives through his motivational teachings.

In addition to teaching, he has composed and sung numerous Sanskrit Bhajans and patriotic songs.

He has also written and directed several short films and documentaries for awareness campaigns, and has volunteered with the police in both UP and Kerala to spread awareness about various issues through videos and photography.

Incredibly, he has produced and directed over 100 documentaries about the city of Varanasi, all on his own.

He has also helped and guided more than 25 boys and girls to achieve world records through creative and innovative methods. He is a multifaceted person who uses his intellect and the blessings given to him by God to excel in various areas. He is both a teacher and a student, always learning and teaching, and is able to master any subject he comes across.

He is a selfless social activist and motivational speaker who has overcome struggles and failures to become a successful and enthusiastic individual with a rich life experience.

In addition to his work with the Bhagavad Gita, he is also an efficient Tarot card reader, Astro-Vastu consultant, and a talented singer and composer. He has sung the entire Ram Charita Manas and Bhagavad Gita in his own compositions, and has sung the phrase "Lokah Samastha Sukhino Bhavantu" in 50 different languages. He is currently working on a detailed and scientific study of Vedas, Upanishads, Puranas, and the Bhagavad Gita. He has also composed and sung the Hanuman Chalisa and Gayatri Mantra in 108 and 1008 different compositions, respectively.

Awards - Four Times Guinness World Records, Winner of Mahatma Gandhi Vishwa Shanti Puraskar, Mahatma Gandhi Global Peace Ambassador, Kashi Ratna Award, Dr. APJ Abdul Kalam Motivational Person of the Year 2017, Mother Teresa Award, Indira Gandhi Priyadarshini Award, Bharat Vikas Ratna Award, Udyog Ratna Award, Vigyan Prasar Award, Poorvanchal Ratn Samman.

ᕈᕈᕈ

Preface

India is a land of diversity and rich cultural heritage. From ancient rock-cut temples to modern skyscrapers, India's art and architecture, festivals, dance and music, religion, cuisine, clothing and textiles, and the traditional family structure, have a rich history reflecting the country's diverse regions, religions, and cultures. However, the cultural diversity of India is not only limited to its geography and religion, but also includes a wide range of indigenous tribes and communities, each with their own unique customs, traditions, languages, and beliefs.

The present book, "A Cultural Mosaic: A Study Of The Diverse Traditions And Customs Of India" aims to provide an in-depth understanding of the diversity of Indian culture, its evolution and its impact on the society. The book delves into the cultural traditions of India, exploring the various aspects of Indian culture, including its art and architecture, festivals, dance and music, religion, cuisine, clothing, textiles, and the traditional family structure. The book also explores the role of colonialism and the impact it had on Indian culture, the caste system and its impact on Indian society, the role of women in Indian culture, the evolution of Indian cinema and the tribal cultures of India.

The book also addresses the challenges that Indian culture faces in the globalized world and the future of Indian culture. It highlights the positive aspects of globalization, such as the spread of Indian culture to other parts of the world and the efforts to preserve and promote traditional Indian culture, as well as the negative impacts of globalization, such as the homogenization of culture and the erosion of traditional customs and practices.

This book is a comprehensive study of the diverse traditions and customs of India, and it is an essential guide for anyone interested in understanding the country's rich heritage and its people. The book is written in a clear and concise manner, making it accessible to a wide range of readers, from students and scholars to tourists and general readers.

ᐅᐅᐅ

"India is not a country, it is a continent." - Rabindranath Tagore

ONE

UNDERSTANDING THE DIVERSITY OF INDIAN CULTURE

India is a land of diverse cultures, traditions, and customs. From the snow-capped Himalayas in the north to the tropical beaches of the south, from the deserts of Rajasthan to the lush green forests of the northeast, India is a melting pot of different languages, religions, and ethnic groups. The country's rich history, spanning back to ancient civilization, has contributed to the development of a unique and diverse culture. This diversity is reflected in everything from the food, clothing, and architecture to the music, dance, and festivals.

The Indian subcontinent is home to several major world religions, including Hinduism, Buddhism, Jainism, Sikhism, and Islam. Each of these religions has had a profound impact on Indian culture and society, shaping the country's beliefs, customs, and practices. For example, Hinduism, the oldest religion in India, is known for its caste system, which divides society into four main categories, and its numerous festivals and rituals. Buddhism, which originated in India, has had a significant impact on the country's art, literature, and architecture. Jainism, another ancient Indian religion, emphasizes non-violence and the importance of self-control. Sikhism, a relatively recent religion, emphasizes equality and the importance of community service. Islam, brought to India by traders and invaders, has had a significant impact on Indian culture, particularly in the areas of food, clothing, and architecture.

India's diversity is also reflected in its many languages. There are over 200 languages spoken in India, with Hindi and English being the most widely spoken. However, the official language of the country is Hindi, and the Constitution of India recognizes 22 scheduled languages. Each language has its own unique script, grammar, and vocabulary, and each has played a role in shaping the country's culture and society.

India's diversity is also reflected in its food. The country is known for its delicious and varied cuisine, which is influenced by the many different regions, religions, and cultures. Each state in India has its own unique dishes, made with local ingredients and cooked in traditional ways. For example, the north Indian cuisine is known for its rich and creamy dishes, such as butter chicken and dal makhani, while the south Indian cuisine is known for its use of coconut and spices, such as sambar and dosa. Indian cuisine is also known for its vegetarian dishes, which are popular among Hindus and Jains, and for its street food, which is enjoyed by people of all ages and backgrounds.

India's diversity is also reflected in its clothing and textiles. Each region in India has its own unique style of dress, made from local fabrics and decorated with traditional embroidery and prints. The traditional Indian attire for men is the dhoti and kurta, while the traditional attire for women is the saree. The saree is a long piece of cloth that is wrapped around the body and is worn with a blouse and a petticoat. The traditional Indian attire is still worn by many people, particularly in rural areas, and is considered to be an important part of Indian culture.

India's diversity is also reflected in its architecture. From the ancient rock-cut temples of the south to the Mughal palaces of the north, Indian architecture is known for its intricate carvings, domes, and arches. The ancient Indian architecture is characterized by the use of stone and wood, while the Mughal architecture is known for its use of marble and sandstone. The British colonial architecture is also visible in many parts of India and is characterized by the use of red brick and stone.

India's diversity is also reflected in its music and dance. The country is known for its rich and diverse musical traditions, which have been influenced by different religions, regions, and cultures. From classical music and dance forms such as Bharatanatyam and Kathak to folk music and dance forms such as Bhangra and Garba, India has a wide range of musical and dance styles. Each style has its own unique instruments, rhythms, and movements, and is an important part of the country's cultural heritage.

It is sure that, India's culture is a unique and diverse mosaic of different traditions, customs, and beliefs. From its rich history and religions, to its many languages and cuisines, India's culture is a reflection of the country's diverse regions, ethnic groups, and communities. Understanding the diversity of Indian culture is essential to appreciating the country's rich heritage and to understanding its people and society. This book, "A Cultural Mosaic: A Study of the Diverse Traditions and Customs of India" aims to explore and understand the diversity of Indian culture and to provide a deeper understanding of the country's rich heritage and traditions.

ᐅᐅᐅ

"India is the cradle of the human race, the birthplace of human speech, the mother of history, the grandmother of legend, and the great grandmother of tradition." - Mark Twain

REGIONAL VARIATIONS IN INDIAN FESTIVALS

India is known for its colorful and vibrant festivals, which are celebrated throughout the year in different regions of the country. These festivals are an important part of Indian culture and reflect the country's diverse traditions, customs, and beliefs.

One of the most widely celebrated festivals in India is Diwali, also known as the "Festival of Lights." This festival is celebrated by Hindus, Jains, and Sikhs and marks the victory of good over evil. It is celebrated in October or November and is characterized by the lighting of diyas (oil lamps) and fireworks. In Northern India, Diwali is celebrated over five days and is marked by the exchange of sweets and gifts, while in Southern India it is celebrated for three days and is marked by the lighting of rangolis (colorful floor designs).

Another widely celebrated festival in India is Holi, also known as the "Festival of Colors." This festival is celebrated by Hindus and marks the arrival of spring and the victory of good over evil. It is celebrated in March and is characterized by the throwing of colored powder and the lighting of bonfires. In Northern India, Holi is celebrated over two days and is marked by the playing of traditional music and dancing, while in Western India it is celebrated for one day and is marked by the exchange of sweets and gifts.

In the southern state of Tamil Nadu, Pongal is celebrated which is a harvest festival. It is celebrated in January and is marked by the cooking of traditional dishes made from new rice and the exchange of sweets and gifts.

In the western state of Gujarat, Navaratri is celebrated which is a festival celebrating the victory of good over evil. It is celebrated over nine days and is marked by the worship of the goddess Durga and the playing of traditional music and dancing.

The festival of Onam is celebrated in the southern state of Kerala, it is a harvest festival and is celebrated over ten days in the month of August or September. It is characterized by the exchange of sweets and gifts, traditional music and dance performances, and the famous snake boat race.

These are just a few examples of the many festivals that are celebrated in India, each with their own unique traditions and customs. Regional variations in Indian festivals reflect the diversity of the country's culture and are an important part of Indian heritage.

❧❧❧

"The beauty of India is that it is a land of contrasts. It is not just one color, it is not just one smell, it is not just one tradition." - A.R. Rahman

THREE

FOLK DANCE AND MUSIC OF INDIA

Folk dance and music are an important part of Indian culture, reflecting the country's diverse traditions, customs, and beliefs. These forms of art are passed down from generation to generation and are deeply rooted in the local communities.

One of the most popular folk dances in India is Bhangra, which originated in the Punjab region. This high-energy dance is performed to the beat of the dhol (a traditional drum) and is characterized by its fast-paced footwork and energetic movements. Bhangra is traditionally performed by men, but in recent years, it has become popular among women as well.

Another popular folk dance in India is Garba, which originated in the Gujarat region. This dance is performed during the Navaratri festival and is characterized by its circular movements and the use of the dandiya (a pair of wooden sticks). Garba is traditionally performed by women, but in recent years, it has become popular among men as well.

In the southern state of Tamil Nadu, Bharatanatyam is a classical dance form that is performed to classical Carnatic music. It is characterized by its grace and fluidity of movements, and is considered to be one of the oldest dance forms in India.

In the eastern state of Odisha, the dance form of Odissi is performed. It is characterized by its sensuous movements and the use of intricate hand gestures, and is considered to be one of the oldest classical dance forms in India.

Folk music in India is also diverse and reflects the country's many regions, religions, and cultures. From the devotional songs of the Bhakti movement to the traditional folk songs of rural communities, Indian folk music is known for its rich melodies, rhythms, and lyrics.

Some examples of Indian folk instruments are Dhol, Dholak, Sitar, Sarod, and Tabla. Each instrument has its own unique sound and is used in different forms of music.

Folk dance and music are an important part of Indian culture and reflect the country's diverse traditions, customs, and beliefs. From Bhangra and Garba to Bharatanatyam and Odissi, Indian folk dance is known for its energy and grace, while Indian folk music is known for its rich melodies and rhythms. Understanding the folk dance and music of India is essential to appreciating the country's rich heritage and to understanding its people and society.

ϪϪϪ

"India is not a poor country. It is a rich country with poor people." - Manmohan Singh"

FOUR

THE ROLE OF RELIGION IN INDIAN CULTURE

Religion plays a significant role in Indian culture and society, shaping the country's beliefs, customs, and practices. India is home to several major world religions, including Hinduism, Buddhism, Jainism, Sikhism, and Islam. Each of these religions has had a profound impact on Indian culture and society, influencing everything from art and literature to architecture and festivals.

Hinduism, the oldest religion in India, is the largest religion in the country and has had the most widespread impact on Indian culture. Hinduism has no single founder, no single scripture, and no fixed set of beliefs. It is a complex religion with many different gods and goddesses and a wide range of beliefs and practices. Many of the festivals and rituals in India are rooted in Hinduism, such as Diwali, Holi, and Navaratri. Hinduism also has a significant impact on the country's art, literature, and architecture, with many of the temples and monuments in India being dedicated to Hindu gods and goddesses.

Buddhism, which originated in India, has had a significant impact on Indian culture and society, particularly in the areas of art, literature, and architecture. The religion's emphasis on non-violence and the importance of self-control has had a lasting impact on Indian society, and many of the country's most famous monuments, such as the Ajanta and Ellora caves, are Buddhist temples.

Jainism, another ancient Indian religion, emphasizes non-violence and the importance of self-control, similar to Buddhism. It has had a significant impact on Indian culture, particularly in the areas of art, literature, and architecture. Many of the temples and monuments in India are dedicated to Jain Tirthankaras.

Sikhism, a relatively recent religion, emphasizes equality and the importance of community service. It has had a significant impact on Indian culture and society, particularly in the areas of art, literature, and architecture. Many of the most famous monuments in India, such as the Golden Temple in Amritsar, are Sikh temples.

Islam, brought to India by traders and invaders, has had a significant impact on Indian culture, particularly in the areas of food, clothing, and architecture. The religion's emphasis on prayer and fasting has had a lasting impact on Indian society, and many of the country's most famous monuments, such as the Taj Mahal, are Islamic.

Exactly, religion plays a significant role in Indian culture and society, shaping the country's beliefs, customs, and practices. From Hinduism to Islam, each religion has had a profound impact on Indian culture, influencing everything from art and literature to architecture and festivals. Understanding the role of religion in Indian culture is essential to appreciating the country's rich heritage and to understanding its people and society.

ᐅᐅᐅ

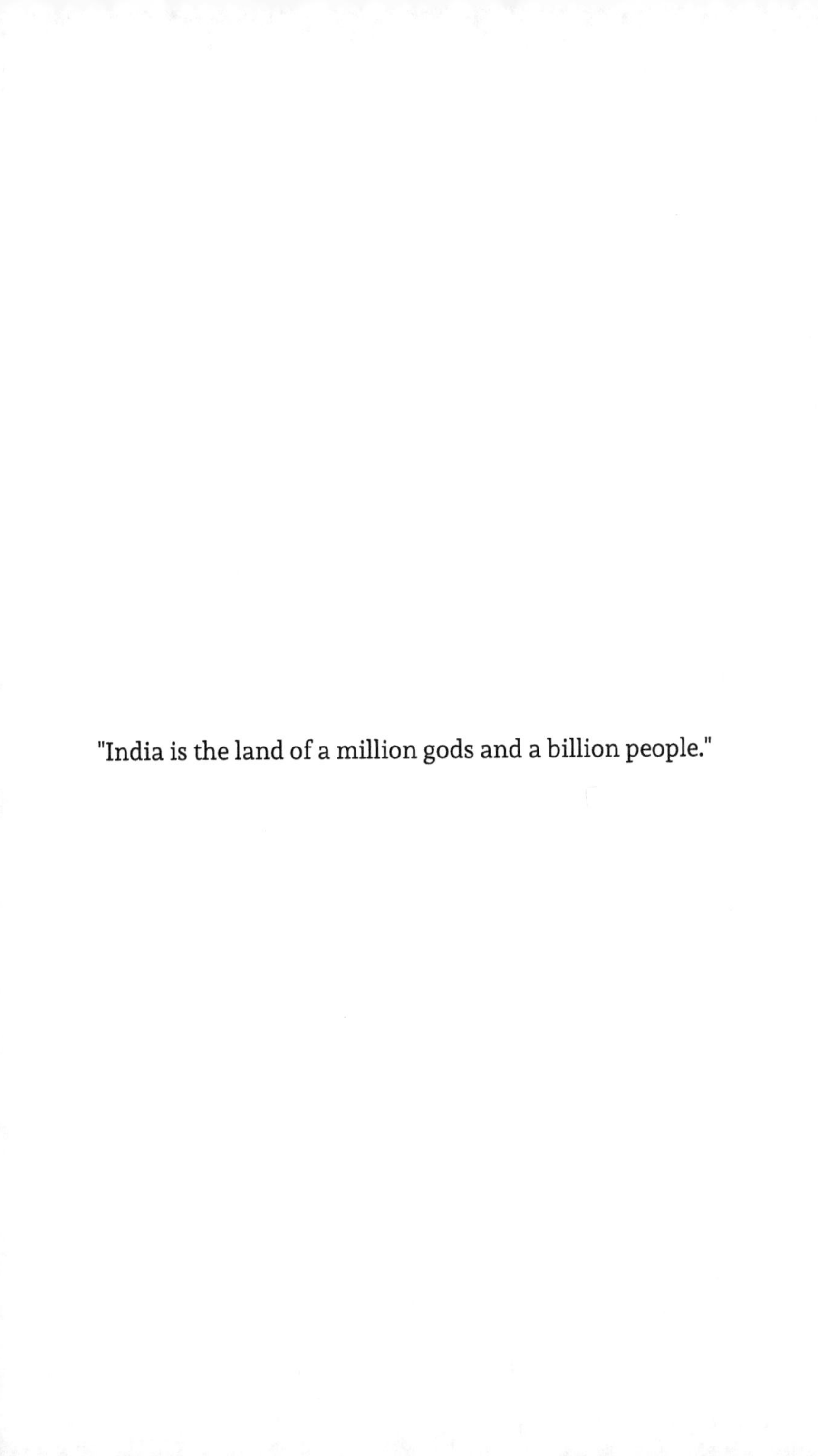

"India is the land of a million gods and a billion people."

FIVE

The Influence of Ancient India on Modern Culture

Ancient India has had a profound influence on modern culture, shaping the country's beliefs, customs, and practices. From its rich history and religions, to its many languages and cuisines, ancient India's culture is still visible in many aspects of modern India.

One of the most notable influences of ancient India on modern culture is in the field of religion. Hinduism, Buddhism, Jainism, and Sikhism, which originated in ancient India, are still practiced in the country today and continue to shape the beliefs and customs of the Indian people. The ancient texts and teachings of these religions, such as the Vedas and Upanishads, continue to be studied and revered in modern India, and many of the country's festivals and rituals are based on ancient traditions.

Ancient India's architecture is also visible in modern culture. The ancient rock-cut temples of the south and the Mughal palaces of the north are still standing today and continue to be visited by millions of tourists each year. The ancient Indian architectural styles, such as the use of stone and wood, the intricate carvings, domes, and arches, continue to inspire modern architects and builders.

Ancient India's contributions to mathematics, astronomy, and medicine are also visible in modern culture. The decimal system and the concept of zero were developed in ancient India, and have had a profound influence on modern mathematics. Indian astronomers of ancient times made significant contributions to the field of astronomy, and the astronomical observations and predictions made in ancient Indian texts are still used today. The Ayurvedic system of medicine, which originated in ancient India, is still widely practiced in the country today and has gained popularity in other parts of the world as well.

Ancient India's literature is also visible in modern culture. The ancient Indian epics such as the Ramayana and the Mahabharata continue to be widely read and performed in modern India and have had a significant influence on the country's literature, art, and popular culture.

Yes, ancient India has had a profound influence on modern culture, shaping the country's beliefs, customs, and practices. From its rich history and religions, to its many languages and cuisines, ancient India's culture is still visible in many aspects of modern India. Understanding the influence of ancient India on modern culture is essential to appreciating the country's rich heritage and to understanding its people and society.

᭥᭥᭥

"India is an old country, but a young nation; I am proud of our ancient heritage, and also of the modern changes wrought by our people." - Jawaharlal Nehru

SIX

INDIAN CUISINE: A MELTING POT OF FLAVORS

Indian cuisine is a melting pot of flavors, reflecting the country's diverse regions, religions, and cultures. From the rich and creamy dishes of the north to the spicy and flavorful dishes of the south, Indian cuisine is known for its delicious and varied flavors.

The north Indian cuisine is known for its rich and creamy dishes, such as butter chicken and dal makhani, which are made with a variety of spices, butter, and cream. These dishes are typically served with naan, a type of leavened bread, and are often accompanied by yogurt-based raita or chutneys. North Indian cuisine is also known for its meat dishes, such as kebabs and biryani, which are made with a variety of meats, including chicken, lamb, and beef.

The south Indian cuisine is known for its use of coconut

and spices, such as sambar and dosa. These dishes are typically served with rice and are often accompanied by chutneys or sambar, a type of lentil-based stew. South Indian cuisine is also known for its vegetarian dishes, such as idli and vada, which are made with a variety of lentils and grains.

The coastal regions of India are known for their seafood dishes such as fish curry, prawn fry, and fish fry. These dishes are made with a variety of fresh seafood and are often flavored with coconut, tamarind, and a variety of spices.

Indian cuisine is also known for its street food, which is enjoyed by people of all ages and backgrounds. From the popular vada pav of Mumbai to the gol gappa of Delhi, Indian street food is known for its delicious and varied flavors.

Indian cuisine is also known for its use of herbs and spices, which play a significant role in adding flavor and aroma to dishes. Commonly used spices in Indian cuisine include cumin, turmeric, coriander, ginger, and chili.

Indian cuisine is a melting pot of flavors, reflecting the country's diverse regions, religions, and cultures. From the rich and creamy dishes of the north to the spicy and flavorful dishes of the south, Indian cuisine is known for its delicious and varied flavors. The use of herbs and spices, as well as the regional variations, make Indian cuisine unique and popular around the world.

ppp

"India is a land of diversity, and that diversity is its beauty."
- L.K. Advani

SEVEN

CLOTHING AND TEXTILES IN INDIA

Clothing and textiles have a rich history in India and are an important part of the country's culture and heritage. From traditional Indian attire to contemporary fashion, the clothing and textiles of India are known for their intricate designs, vibrant colors, and fine craftsmanship.

The traditional Indian attire for men is the dhoti and kurta, which is worn on formal occasions and festivals. The dhoti is a piece of cloth that is wrapped around the waist and legs, while the kurta is a long, loose shirt. This attire is typically made from cotton or silk and is often decorated with intricate embroidery or prints.

The traditional Indian attire for women is the saree, which is worn on formal occasions and festivals. The saree is a long piece of cloth that is wrapped around the body and is worn with a blouse and a petticoat. This attire is typically made from silk, cotton, or other fabrics and is often decorated with intricate embroidery or prints.

In recent times, Indian fashion has also evolved and there are many designers who blend traditional techniques with modern designs. Some of the popular modern Indian clothing includes salwar kameez, lehenga choli, anarkali suits and fusion wear which are a combination of traditional and western styles.

India is also known for its textiles, which are made from a variety of natural fibers, such as cotton, silk, and wool. These textiles are known for their intricate designs, vibrant colors, and fine craftsmanship. Some of the most famous textiles from India include Banarasi silk, Kanchipuram silk, and Kota Doria. The traditional designs and fabrics used to create clothing bespeak the country's cultural heritage and make it one of the most fascinating apparel markets in the world.

Over recent decades, the Indian fashion industry has grown tremendously due to liberalization policies of the government which have helped spur innovation and growth within this sector. In fact, many textile manufacturers in India are now producing trendy western-style wear with updated cuts and colorful prints. Clothes made from iconic Indian materials such as Khadi fabric, block printed cotton and silk remain popular throughout India but also abroad, especially in countries home to large populations of Indian descendants. It is thus safe to say that Indian textiles will continue to be celebrated around the world for years to come.

❦❦❦

"India is a land of wonder, a land of mystery, a land of inspiration." - David Lean

EIGHT

THE ART AND ARCHITECTURE OF INDIA

The art and architecture of India have a rich history, reflecting the country's diverse regions, religions, and cultures. From ancient rock-cut temples to modern skyscrapers, Indian art and architecture are known for their intricate designs, vibrant colors, and fine craftsmanship.

One of the most notable examples of ancient Indian art and architecture is the rock-cut temples of the south. These temples were carved out of solid rock and are known for their intricate carvings and sculptures. Some of the most famous rock-cut temples in India include the Ajanta and Ellora caves, which feature elaborate carvings and sculptures of gods and goddesses.

Another example of ancient Indian art and architecture is

the Mughal palaces of the north. These palaces were built during the Mughal Empire and are known for their grandeur and elegance. Some of the most famous Mughal palaces in India include the Taj Mahal, the Red Fort, and the Agra Fort, which feature intricate carvings, marble inlays, and beautiful gardens.

In modern times, Indian architecture has also evolved and there are many architects who blend traditional techniques with modern designs. Some of the popular modern Indian architecture includes the Lotus Temple, the Mumbai International Airport, and the Indian Institute of Technology in Delhi.

Indian art is also known for its rich tradition, including miniature paintings, sculptures, and textiles. Indian miniature paintings are known for their intricate details, vibrant colors, and the use of gold and silver. Indian sculptures are known for their intricate carvings, and the use of various materials like stone, metal, and wood. Indian textiles are known for their intricate designs, vibrant colors, and fine craftsmanship.

Surely, the art and architecture of India have a rich history, reflecting the country's diverse regions, religions, and cultures. From ancient rock-cut temples to modern skyscrapers, Indian art and architecture are known for their intricate designs, vibrant colors, and fine craftsmanship. Understanding the art and architecture of India is essential to appreciating the country's rich heritage and to understanding its people and society.

ϼϼϼ

"India is a place where the past, present, and future all exist together."

NINE

THE IMPACT OF COLONIALISM ON INDIAN CULTURE

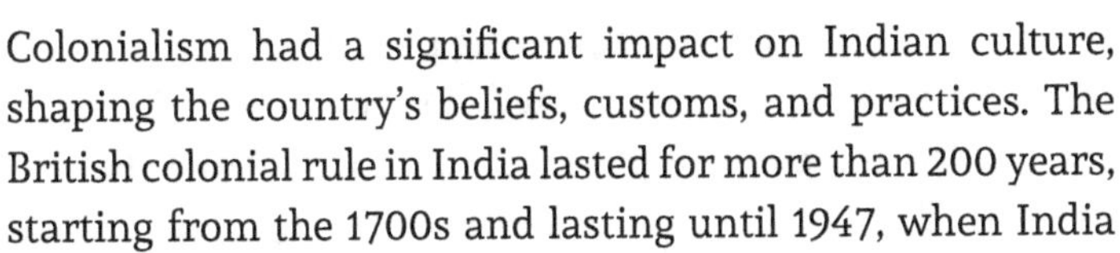

Colonialism had a significant impact on Indian culture, shaping the country's beliefs, customs, and practices. The British colonial rule in India lasted for more than 200 years, starting from the 1700s and lasting until 1947, when India gained its independence.

During colonial rule, the British introduced Western customs, beliefs, and practices to India, which had a lasting impact on the country's culture. For example, the British introduced Western education and legal systems, which greatly influenced the development of modern India. The British also introduced Western concepts such as individualism, rationalism, and secularism, which had a lasting impact on Indian society and culture.

The British also had a significant impact on Indian

economy and trade. They introduced new crops such as tea, opium, and cotton, which greatly changed the agricultural landscape of India. They also introduced a new system of land revenue and land ownership, which had a lasting impact on Indian society and economy.

The British also had a significant impact on Indian art and architecture. They introduced new styles and techniques, such as the Gothic style, which greatly influenced the development of modern Indian architecture. The British also had a significant impact on Indian literature, introducing new styles and forms of writing, such as the novel, which greatly influenced the development of modern Indian literature.

In addition, the British, during their rule, had a significant impact on the caste system, which was an integral part of Indian society, by implementing policies that reinforced the caste system and perpetuated discrimination. They also introduced the concept of racial hierarchy, which further reinforced caste-based discrimination and led to the marginalization of certain communities.

Moreover, British colonialism had a significant impact on the Indian identity, culture and language. They imposed English as the language of administration, education and trade. This led to the decline of traditional Indian languages and the erosion of traditional cultural practices.

Colonialism had a significant impact on Indian culture, shaping the country's beliefs, customs, and practices. The British colonial rule in India, which lasted for more than 200 years, introduced Western customs, beliefs, and practices to India, which had a lasting impact on the country's culture, economy, art and architecture, literature, and society. The British also had a significant impact on the caste system and the Indian identity, culture and language. Understanding the impact of colonialism on Indian culture is essential to understand the country's history and its people, as well as its present.

❦❦❦

"In India, I found a race of mortals living upon the Earth,
but not adhering to it." - Ralph Waldo Emerson

TEN

THE TRADITIONAL INDIAN FAMILY STRUCTURE

The traditional Indian family structure is characterized by strong patriarchal and patrilineal values, with a hierarchical system of authority and decision-making. The family is considered the basic unit of society and is closely knit, with a strong emphasis on loyalty, obedience and respect for elders.

The head of the traditional Indian family is the patriarch, usually the father or the eldest male member of the family. He is the main decision-maker and is responsible for the well-being of the family. The patriarch is also responsible for maintaining the honor and reputation of the family.

The traditional Indian family is also characterized by a

joint family system, where multiple generations of a family live together under one roof. The eldest male member, usually the patriarch, is the head of the joint family and is responsible for its well-being. The joint family system provides a strong support system for its members, and is considered an important aspect of Indian culture.

The traditional Indian family places a strong emphasis on marriage, which is considered a sacred bond between two individuals and their families. Arranged marriages are still common in traditional Indian families and are seen as a way to strengthen family ties and maintain cultural traditions.

The traditional Indian family also places a strong emphasis on the role of women, who are expected to be submissive and obedient to men, especially to their husbands and fathers-in-law. Women are also expected to take care of the household and raise children.

No doubt, the traditional Indian family structure is characterized by strong patriarchal and patrilineal values, with a hierarchical system of authority and decision-making. The family is considered the basic unit of society and is closely knit, with a strong emphasis on loyalty, obedience and respect for elders. The joint family system and arranged marriages are also considered an important aspect of Indian culture. However, with the changes in society and economy, the traditional family structure has been evolving and some aspects of it may not be as prominent as they once were.

ꗞꗞꗞ

"India is the meeting place of the religions and among these Hinduism alone is by itself a vast and complex thing, not so much a religion as a great diversified and yet subtly unified mass of spiritual thought, realization and aspiration." - Sri Aurobindo

ELEVEN

THE CASTE SYSTEM AND ITS IMPACT ON INDIAN SOCIETY

The caste system is a social hierarchy that has been a part of Indian society for centuries. It is based on the belief in the inherent and unchangeable nature of individuals, and their placement in a hierarchical system based on birth. The caste system is traditionally divided into four main categories known as varnas, which are: Brahmins (priests and scholars), Kshatriyas (warriors and rulers), Vaishyas (merchants and traders) and Shudras (servants and laborers).

The caste system has had a significant impact on Indian society, shaping the country's beliefs, customs, and practices. It has been used to justify social and economic inequality and discrimination, with certain castes being deemed as "high" or "low" based on their place in the hierarchy. This has led to the marginalization and oppression of certain castes, particularly those considered "low" or "untouchable."

The caste system has also had a significant impact on Indian economy and politics. It has been used to justify economic inequality, with certain castes being denied access to education, jobs, and other economic opportunities. In addition, the caste system has been used to justify political inequality, with certain castes being denied access to political power and representation.

The caste system has also had a significant impact on Indian art and culture. It has been used to justify the marginalization of certain artists and cultural traditions, and to reinforce the dominance of certain cultural practices and beliefs.

The caste system has been challenged and reformed over time, with legislation and policy changes aimed at eliminating discrimination and promoting equality. However, it continues to shape Indian society, and its effects are still visible today.

Finally, the caste system is a social hierarchy that has been a part of Indian society for centuries, it has had a significant impact on Indian society, shaping the country's beliefs, customs, and practices. It has been used to justify social and economic inequality and discrimination, and has led to the marginalization and oppression of certain castes. The caste system continues to shape Indian society and its effects are still visible today.

ᗐᗐᗐ

"India has a way of mesmerizing you, captivating you, and fascinating you. There's a magic to India that's hard to explain." - Anthony Bourdain

TWELVE

THE ROLE OF WOMEN IN INDIAN CULTURE

The role of women in Indian culture has undergone significant changes over time, with traditional patriarchal values and customs still influencing the status and rights of women in the country. Historically, women in India have been expected to be submissive and obedient to men, with a primary focus on their roles as daughters, wives, and mothers.

Traditionally, Indian society has placed a strong emphasis on the role of women in the domestic sphere, with women being responsible for the care of the home and the family. This includes tasks such as cooking, cleaning, and raising children. Women were also expected to be chaste and virtuous, with their reputation and honor being closely tied to their unethical conduct.

In recent years, there has been a significant shift in the role of women in Indian culture, with more women pursuing education and entering the workforce. There has also been a growing awareness and acceptance of women's rights and equality, with movements and initiatives aimed at promoting gender equality and challenging traditional patriarchal values.

However, despite these changes, women in India still face significant challenges and discrimination. They continue to be underrepresented in leadership positions, and are more likely to be illiterate and poor than men. Women also face significant violence, including domestic abuse, unethical assault and harassment.

The role of women in Indian culture has undergone significant changes over time, with traditional patriarchal values and customs still influencing the status and rights of women in the country. Women in India have traditionally been expected to be submissive and obedient to men, with a primary focus on their roles as daughters, wives, and mothers. However, in recent years, there has been a significant shift in the role of women in Indian culture, with more women pursuing education and entering the workforce. Despite these changes, women in India still face significant challenges and discrimination.

ᕱᕱᕱ

"India is a land of ancient civilization and culture, where tradition and modernity coexist in perfect harmony." - Dalai Lama

THIRTEEN

THE EVOLUTION OF INDIAN CINEMA

Indian cinema, also known as Bollywood, has undergone significant evolution over the years. The cinema industry of India has come a long way, and it has had a positive impact on the country's culture and society.

One of the positive aspects of the evolution of Indian cinema is the representation of diverse stories and characters. Indian cinema has traditionally focused on mainstream, commercial storylines, but in recent years, there has been a growing trend of independent and alternative cinema that represents a diverse range of stories and characters, including those from underrepresented communities.

Another positive aspect of the evolution of Indian cinema is the increasing representation of women in leading roles and behind the camera. Historically, Indian cinema has been male-dominated, both in front of and behind the camera. But in recent years, there has been a growing number of female filmmakers and female-led stories, which has helped to challenge gender stereotypes and promote gender equality.

Additionally, Indian cinema has evolved to become a significant cultural export, gaining popularity in other countries and helping to promote Indian culture and values on a global scale. The industry has also created a lot of jobs and economic opportunities for people from all walks of life.

Lastly, Indian cinema has been a source of entertainment for many people around the country, and it has helped to bring together people of different backgrounds and cultures. It has been a powerful medium for the expression of emotions and ideas, and has contributed to the cultural fabric of the country.

Indian cinema has undergone significant evolution over the years, with a positive impact on the country's culture and society. The representation of diverse stories and characters, increasing representation of women, becoming a significant cultural export, creating jobs and economic opportunities and being a source of entertainment for people around the country are some of the positive aspects of the evolution of Indian cinema.

ᐅᐅᐅ

"India is a country of many languages and many religions, but it is also a country of many beautiful landscapes and many beautiful buildings." - Gustave Flaubert

FOURTEEN

TRIBAL CULTURES OF INDIA

The tribal cultures of India are diverse and rich, representing the country's indigenous populations. These cultures have their own unique customs, traditions, languages, and beliefs, which have been passed down through generations.

Tribal cultures in India are primarily found in the northeastern and central regions of the country, with the largest concentration in the states of Orissa, Jharkhand, Chhattisgarh, and Maharashtra. These tribes have their own distinct languages, customs, and traditions, which have been shaped by their environment and their history.

One of the most notable aspects of tribal cultures in India is their relationship with nature. Many tribes have a deep spiritual connection to the land and its natural resources, and their customs and traditions are closely tied to the environment. This is reflected in their art, music, and rituals, which often feature elements of nature.

Tribal cultures in India are also known for their rich oral traditions, which are passed down through generations. These traditions include stories, songs, and folktales that reflect the tribe's history, beliefs, and customs.

In recent years, tribal cultures in India have been facing challenges, such as displacement and loss of land, due to development projects. In addition, they also face challenges related to poverty, lack of education, and discrimination.

The tribal cultures of India are diverse and rich, representing the country's indigenous populations. These cultures have their own unique customs, traditions, languages, and beliefs, which have been passed down through generations. The relationship with nature, rich oral traditions and the challenges faced by these cultures are some of the most notable aspects of tribal cultures in India. It is important to preserve and promote these cultures as they are an important part of India's heritage and identity.

ᑭᑭᑭ

"India is a land of many wonders, a land of many
contrasts, a land of many mysteries." - Paul Theroux

FIFTEEN

THE FUTURE OF INDIAN CULTURE IN THE GLOBALIZED WORLD

The Indian culture has been around for more than 5000 years and has been strongly characterized by its great diversity in religions, languages, cultures and lifestyles. In the modern world, we see India process an outside force of globalization and this trend has had a major impact on the Indian culture. Globalization has brought with it new technologies, communication, and methods of transportation, leading to an ever-growing contact across multiple continents and cultures.

The introduction of foreign influences has had a major

effect on Indian culture in terms of language, food, dress and other popular culture aspects. Recently, India was introduced to new westernized trends and fashions, which have been readily accepted by the people and are now part of the national culture. In addition to this, the language used in advertisements and the media has become increasingly westernized. Similarly, many Indian cities have come to adopt western-style infrastructure, and it is no longer uncommon to find multistory glass and concrete buildings in Indian cities.

Although these western changes have had a significant impact on traditional Indian culture, some things remain unchanged. Indian religions, for example, are still thriving and a central part of the culture. The regional flavor of traditional Indian foods, music, and festivals are also still held with great reverence in Indian communities, which has been bolstered through digital media. Moreover, while English is making its place in the Indian literary culture, regional languages such as Hindi and Bengali are still holding their ground.

As the world continues its march towards globalization, India's culture will be increasingly molded by foreign forces. Despite its westernization, India still has a very vibrant and diverse cultural heritage rooted in old traditions, values and identities. In the future, India may look very different in terms of lifestyles, technology, and industry, but traditional Indian culture will still exist and be admired. The history and religion that was so important to previous generations will continue to be important to Indians of the future, albeit in different ways and contexts. In a globalized world, Indians can remain linked to their culture and their identity even as the world around them has changed.

It is difficult to predict the exact future of Indian culture in a globalized world. However, it is likely that Indian culture will continue to have a significant impact on the global stage. As more people around the world are exposed to Indian culture through travel, media, and the internet, it is likely that elements of Indian culture will continue to be adopted and integrated into other cultures. Additionally, as India continues to develop economically and politically, it will likely play an increasingly important role in shaping the global cultural landscape. However, it is also important to note that globalization can also have negative impacts on traditional cultures, leading to homogenization and the loss of unique cultural practices and traditions.

Other Book Of The Author

1. The Moments When I Met God
2. Kashiyile Theertha Pathangal
3. GURU GYAN VANI
4. Abhiprerak Gita
5. ASSI SE JAIN GHAT TAK
6. Hopelessness of Arjuna
7. The Soul and It's True Nature
8. Sense of Action (Karma)
9. Action through Wisdom
10. Action through Wisdom
11. THEORY AND PRACTICAL OF EVERY ACTION
12. LOGICAL UNDERSTANDING OF THE SUPREME
13. THE IMPERISHABLE SUPREME
14. Yatra Nishadraj se Hanuman Ghat Tak
15. Yatra Karnatak Ghat se Raja Ghat Tak
16. Yatra Pandey Ghat se Prayagraj Ghat Tak
17. Yatra Ranjendra Prasad Ghat se Dattatreya Ghat Tak
18. YaatraSindhiya Ghat se Gwaliar Ghat Tak
19. Yatra Mangala Gauri Ghat se Hanuman Gadhi Ghat Tak
20. Yatra Gaay Ghat Se Nishad Ghat Tak
21. MAA GANGA, GHATEN EVM UTSAV
22. Ganga Arti Dev Deepavali evam Any Utsav
23. Potentials of Digitalized India
24. VEDIC CONSCIOUSNESS
25. A Brief Introduction to Vedic Science
26. Kashi ke Barah Jyotirling
27. IMPACT OF MOTIVATION
28. Let's have a Milky Way Journey
29. Color Therapy in a Nutshell

30. Rigveda in a Nutshell
31. Yajurveda in a Nutshell
32. Samveda in a Nutshell
33. Atharva Veda in a Nutshell
34. Ayushman Bhava - Ayurveda
35. Srimad Bhagavad Gita and Upanishad Connection
36. Srimad Bhagavad Gita - an attempt to summarize each chapter.
37. Facts and Impact of Nakshatra
38. Astro Gems - NAVARATNA
39. Ekadashi - A Concise Overview
40. A Concise View of Hanuman Chalisa
41. Inspirational Gita
42. Nakshatraranyam
43. Summary of 18 Mahapuranas
44. Synopsis of 18 Upa Puranas
45. Rigvediya Upanishads
46. Shukla Yajurvediya Upanishads
47. Krishna Yajurvediya Upanishads
48. Samavediya Upanishads
49. Atharvavediya Upanishads
50. The Seven Great Sages
51. From Rocket Scientist to President Dr. APJ Abdul Kalam
52. The Visionary's Voice - Quotes of Dr. APJ Abdul Kalam
53. The Wisdom of Swami Vivekananda: Insights and Inspiration from a Legendary Spiritual Teacher
54. Ayurvedic Remedies from the Garden
55. Sages and Seers
56. Rising Strong – Motivational Stories of Women
57. Beyond Flames -Mystery stories of Funeral Ghat Manikarnika
58. The Origins of Tulsi: A Look at the Mythological Roots of the Plant"

ॐॐॐ

Contact

DR. JAGADEESH PILLAI

PhD in Vedic Science

Four Times Guinness World Record Holder

Winner of Mahatma Gandhi Vishwa Shanti Puraskar and
Global Peace Ambassador

Gemology, Astro & Vastu Consultant - Spiritual Counselor

Consultant for designing World Record Ideas

Efficient Tarot Card Reader

9839093003

myrichindia@gmail.com

drjagadeeshpillai@facebook

drjagadeeshpillai@instagram

jagadeeshpillai@youtube

www. JAGADEESHPILLAI.com

❦❦❦

|| LOKAHA SAMASTHAHA SUKHINO BHAVANTU ||

• 85 •

www.ingramcontent.com/pod-product-compliance
Lightning Source LLC
Chambersburg PA
CBHW061658130726

47996CB00006B/2085